MECCA

Roger Marriott

SHIRE PUBLICATIONS

Published in Great Britain in 2012 by Shire Publications
Ltd, Midland House, West Way, Botley, Oxford OX2 0PH,
United Kingdom.

44-02 23rd Street, Suite 219, Long Island City, NY 11101,
USA.

E-mail: shire@shirebooks.co.uk   www.shirebooks.co.uk

A CIP catalogue record for this book is available from the
British Library.

Shire Library no. 653.   ISBN-13: 978 0 74781 056 8

Roger Marriott has asserted his right under the Copyright,
Designs and Patents Act, 1988, to be identified as the
author of this book.

Designed by Tony Truscott Designs, Sussex, UK
and typeset in Perpetua and Gill Sans.

Printed in China through Worldprint Ltd.

12 13 14 15 16   10 9 8 7 6 5 4 3 2 1

COVER IMAGE
Detail of the advertisement on page 60.

TITLE PAGE IMAGE
A shop display card from the early 1950s showing the
iconic giant block-setting crane.

CONTENTS PAGE IMAGE
The revised Meccano chassis based on the Bentley 'silent
sports car' of 1933, the only new Supermodel leaflet to ▯
prepared especially for the blue and gold set L (see page
45). Demonstration model built by the author.

ACKNOWLEDGEMENTS
I am grateful to Jim Gamble for suggesting that I should
write this book, and for his help and permission to use
photographs of items from his collection at the Meccano
Museum in Nottingham. I would especially like to thank
Robin Johnson of Constructor Quarterly for his meticulous
proofreading and his many helpful suggestions. I would
also like to acknowledge the help of Malcolm Hanson, T▯
McCallum and Robin Johnson of Constructor Quarterly, w▯
have given permission for the publication of many of the
illustrations. Other illustrations are taken from the Mecc▯
Magazine and Meccano publicity material and instructio▯
books and photographs by the author. It has not been
possible in every case to trace the copyright holders.

Illustrations are acknowledged as follows:

Constructor Quarterly, pages 17, 23, 25, 33, 36, 38, 39, 4▯
41, 42 and 48; Jim Gamble, pages 10, 14, 19, 64; Malc▯
Hanson, pages 11, 24, 27, 43, 44, 46, 45, 48, 52, 53, 5▯
55, 57, 58, 63 and 71; John Thorpe, page 77.

Shire Publications is supporting the Woodland Trust, the UK's leading woodland conservation charity, by funding the dedication of trees.

CONTENTS

MECCANO

Miniature Engineerin for Boy

NTRODUCTION

T HE STORY OF MECCANO is the story of five generations of boys who found enjoyment in a toy that taught the principles of mechanics and enabled em (and a few girls) to make things that really worked. It is a story that flects the development of technology for almost a century. In 1900 Great 'itain was a world power and an industrial nation that exported to a orldwide empire. Its industrial success was largely based upon the inciples of mechanical engineering and steam power. The motor car was out to change society, as the railways had done fifty years earlier; electricity as an embryonic technology, but civil and mechanical engineering were ansforming the world. Around 1900, when Frank Hornby had the idea of onstructional toy to amuse his two young sons, he visualised an educational y that would enable them to understand the principles of engineering and ake engineering famous to millions of other boys worldwide.

'Meccano' has entered the dictionary as a term in common usage, even ough it is no longer the everyday toy that once almost every boy owned. rents wanted their sons to become responsible, useful citizens with orthwhile, productive careers, and were persuaded by subtle advertising t their boys needed only Meccano to become successful engineers. This is story behind the illustrations on Meccano instruction books and set boxes the 1940s and 1950s, showing a pipe-smoking father looking over his sons' rk with obvious approval.

Frank Hornby was born into a middle-class Victorian family in 1863 and cated at the Liverpool High School for Boys, a mechanics institute founded the training of engineers. As a young man he would have seen the prosperity Great Britain and would have been impressed by the achievements of great gineers such as I. K. Brunel. The late nineteenth century was an age of viously unprecedented engineering achievement. Hornby considered a eer in engineering but this apparently did not suit him and he was sent into iness by his family. His father being a provisions wholesaler, Frank would bably have begun his career with the family business. He eventually became ef cashier for David Hugh Elliott, a Liverpool shipping merchant, but he

Opposite:
A typical shop display card from the 1960s showing industrious Meccano civil engineers constructing a famous bridge.

5

The evocative cover designed by W. H. Pinyon for Meccano instruction manuals in the 1950s.

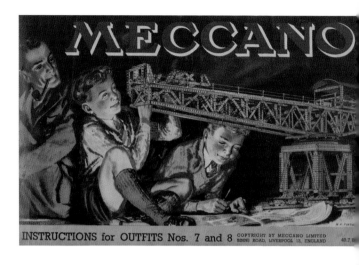

INSTRUCTIONS for OUTFITS Nos. 7 and 8 COPYRIGHT BY MECCANO LIMITED BINNS ROAD, LIVERPOOL 13, ENGLAND

always retained an interest in engineering, and, while on a train journey, had an idea for an educational toy to teach boys the principles of mechanical engineering. Thirty years later, when writing the story of his invention in the *Meccano Magazine*, he recalled the occasion:

> One snowy Christmas Eve I was making a long railway journey and as I sat in my corner seat my mind was as usual turning over new schemes for my boys' enjoyment. At that time we were experiencing trouble in our little workshop through lack of a number of small parts for building a splendid model crane... I felt that what was required was parts that could be applied in different ways to many different models and that could be adjusted to give a variety of movements...

The invention was not totally original, as other toy construction systems had been made, but Hornby's had the key characteristic of using interchangeable metal strips that could be bolted together through holes spaced at fixed intervals, enabling strong and rigid structures to be easily built. The key feature of the invention was a standard building unit of a $\frac{1}{2}$ inch-wide metal strip, with fixing holes spaced every $\frac{1}{2}$ inch along the length of the strip. Hornby also realised the value of having an odd number of holes, thus providing a central fixing point, and so the strips were initially produced in three lengths: $2\frac{1}{2}$ inches, $5\frac{1}{2}$ inches and $12\frac{1}{2}$ inches. Using elongated holes on angle pieces enabled adjustment to be made when joining strips and girders together. The standard dimensions of the pieces and the use of $\frac{5}{?}$ inch BSW (British Standard Whitworth) nuts and bolts have remained unchanged to this day.

6

Following the advice of his employer, D. H. Elliott, Hornby patented
is invention. Some years later, he recalled the setting of his first patent:

> I claim that Meccano is the original application of the basic principles of
> engineering to a metal constructional or mechanical toy. It was on this
> basis ... that I obtained the first patent for my invention, on 9th January
> 1901. (*Meccano Magazine*, 1932)

› this way was invented the toy that would change Frank Hornby's life
1d the lives of many boys in the twentieth century, and that created a
orld of engineering in miniature.

From that initial idea and the invention of a small range of parts,
1e Meccano system developed into a comprehensive range of sets
›er the next eighty years. The range of parts, some highly specialised,
‹panded to enable increasingly complex models to be built. The basic
inciples would remain the same but the presentation of the parts and sets
‹uld change dramatically. Parts were initially tin plated, then nickel plated;
‹e introduction of painted parts in the mid-1920s was followed by changes
colour scheme, reconfiguration of sets, and a gradual reduction in the
1ge and size of sets until the collapse of British Meccano in 1979.

Mechanics Made
Easy instruction
book, c. 1906.
(Courtesy of
James G Gamble.)

A crane similar
to the example
in Hornby's
original patent and
showing the first
type of 'Meccano'
parts.

MECHANICS MADE EASY' TO 'MECCANO': 1901–8

'NITIALLY CALLED 'Mechanics Made Easy', the first sets of 1901 had a very limited range of parts. At first, all the parts were bought in, manufactured / other firms, and throughout these early years the strips and girders were ry crudely made. (High-quality production did not begin until Hornby oved to the new factory in Binns Road, Liverpool, in 1914.) However, ornby realised that packaging and presentation were vital to the success of s products, and so the tins containing the parts were attractively tin-printed.

By 1904 the range of parts had expanded to include girders and gear heels. There were three main boxes, A, B and C, and a box of accessories, 1. The outfits were expensive: the smallest set, Box A, was priced at 8s 6d, hen the average weekly wage for a skilled engineer was around £2 to £2)s. However, through astute marketing, building on the educational pirations of middle-class families, and capitalising on his contact with a verpool University professor, H. S. Hele-Shaw, Mechanics Made Easy tablished a foothold in the developing British toy market.

At some time before 1904 Hornby developed a marketing strategy that rved extremely well for the next seventy years. Each set was complete in elf and associated with a group of models described in the instruction anual. The outfits were also progressive: the A set could be converted into 3 set by the purchase of a connecting outfit, A1. These 'accessory' outfits ter becoming 1a, 2a, etc.) enabled nearly every household to own a eccano set and encouraged boys to dream of gradually acquiring the largest : through birthday and Christmas presents.

Until 1905, even the largest box, C, priced at £1 4s 6d, did not contain ge quantities of parts, and so the models in the manuals were relatively mentary. The first model-building competition, advertised in the *Model jineer* in 1904, provided a range of new and more advanced models. Entries the competition included models of famous Victorian structures such as the rth Bridge, the original of which was built entirely of steel and completed 1890. This was an ideal subject for a Meccano model and Hornby was atly impressed by the model entered by Bedford Grammar School.

Opposite:
Meccano No. 1
outfit of 1908,
showing the new
design of carton
and instruction
manual.

Top: An early Mechanics Made Easy set, set A. Note the attractive tin printing, with the inclusion of Elliott's name and the James Street address. (Courtesy of James G Gamble.)

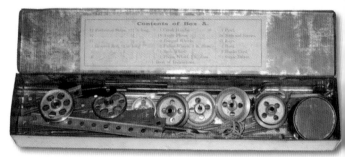

Middle: An example of the accessory box A1 for converting set A into set B. This principle was key to the success of Meccano, enabling boys to expand their set gradually into the largest. (Courtesy of James G. Gamble.)

Bottom: Box X was the first 'starter set', but, priced at 5s, it was still expensive.

o enable it to be built, he extended the number of sets to include the first
uper' outfit, the massive E box.

Model-building competitions were a rich source of model plans and were
useful advertisement. Hornby used the prize-winning models to great effect
his advertising to inspire boys and their fathers to build larger and more
npressive models – and so to purchase larger quantities of parts.

The 1906–7 manual illustrates the latest range of parts, most now with
umbers, and includes a price list showing boxes A to E and a starter set, box
. Box X, contained in a cardboard carton, provided parts to make eight
odels and was priced at 5s; it was an early junior set.

In 1907 the business was sufficiently successful to support a move from its
riginal premises in James Street to larger premises in Duke Street, Liverpool,
abling Hornby to set up a proper manufacturing facility. On 14 September
that year the tradename 'Meccano' was registered, but it was not until 1908
at the new company of Meccano Ltd came into being. Until then Hornby
d been in partnership with his old employer, David Hugh Elliott – hence the
onogram E&H (or Elliott & Hornby) on Mechanics Made Easy boxes.
owever, Elliott did not become a shareholder in the Meccano company,
ossibly because his health was failing.

The origin of the name 'Meccano' is unclear. Jim Gamble, in his book on
ank Hornby, recounts that various Meccano employees claimed that the
ord was invented by Hornby as a contraction of 'make and know', but
quotes Hornby himself: 'I decided on the
me because it was one that people of every
tionality could pronounce.'

The first set to bear the 'Meccano' name
s the Kindergarten outfit, produced
obably for Christmas 1907. The manual
rried the title 'Kindergarten Drawing Book'
d in brackets 'Mechanics Made Easy'.
ornby continued to use the by then well-
own name 'Mechanics Made Easy' as a
btitle well into the Meccano era, not
pping it until 1911. The Kindergarten set,
ich remained on the market until 1910,
ntinued the successful emphasis on
ucation by encouraging children to draw
t simple models on squared paper in the
wing book before construction. The parts
re still of the same construction as
chanics Made Easy parts – tinplate strips
h folded edges.

The first set
to carry the
'Meccano' title,
the Kindergarten
outfit of 1907, still
with Mechanics
Made Easy design
parts.

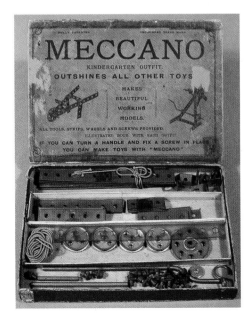

MECCANO

100 TOYS IN ONE

MECCANO 1908–18

N 1908 a number of fundamental changes occurred. Hornby had adopted correct engineering principles for his early parts, using slotted rods with ryways, and gears with saw-cut slots to take the keys. In practice, these atures were not well suited to a children's toy and were gradually spensed with, firstly by modification to the keys in 1908–9, and entually by the introduction of bosses with set screws in 1911. Hornby .d employed a qualified engineer in his new factory and now had the pability to manufacture parts to his own specification. The folded-over -plated strips were replaced by more substantial nickel-plated rolled :el, and the brass wheels and gears were turned rather than bought in as st items.

Meccano outfits were now denoted by numbers rather than letters, and ntained in well-made cardboard cartons instead of litho-printed tins. .anuals and cartons carried attractive eye-catching graphics showing a happy ·y and girl about to embark on the construction of a wide range of models. ıe established slogan of 'Best Boy's Toy' is prominently displayed, despite e inclusion of a girl on the cover. This feature was to be short-lived: :ccano sets did not carry a girl's image again for over sixty years.

Although the new manuals were very well produced on good-quality art per, the models illustrated were largely reproduced from the old :chanics Made Easy manual, with little change to reflect the modified rts, but the larger pages and landscape format (9¾ by 7 inches) allowed the lusion of building instructions and educational notes.

By the end of 1908 a new style of manual and carton was introduced ıt remained essentially the same until the mid-1930s. The boxes, initially th a matchbox style of opening, were covered in black paper with a brightly oured Meccano label. The Mechanics Made Easy subtitle no longer peared on the boxes but was retained on the manual cover until 1911–12. transporter bridge, probably inspired by the new bridge built linking dnes and Runcorn over the Manchester Ship Canal in 1905 (the first nsporter bridge in Britain), was now included in the manuals.

Opposite:
An early shop
display card
probably for the
American market,
c. 1910.

Better-quality parts produced by the new Meccano factory at Duke Street, Liverpool (1908). The new rolled, nickel-plated perforated strips replaced the early tin-plated folded-edge strips.

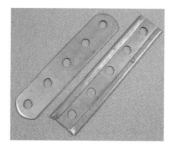

Meccano set, c. 1910. Notice the subtle change in the lettering of the word 'Meccano'. The label shows a boy constructing a crane, and a number of line drawings of models, including a transporter bridge. The manual still carries the subtitle 'Mechanics Made Easy'.

Between 1908 and 1912 five different manuals of instructions, 'for the whole series of models comprising eleven progressive outfits', were published. Supplementary instructions gradually extended the range of models and reflected developments in technology. One supplement from 1909 shows how up-to-date Meccano was, capitalising on the excitement generated by the achievements of the pioneering aviators the Wright brothers with a model of their 'Flyer'. Added realism was provided by the introduction of aeroplane blades. Plates were not included in the system until 1910 and, as with other large models, Hornby suggested using cardboard to fill in the framework.

The largest sets, Nos. 5 and 6, were available in presentation cabinets described in a contemporary advertising leaflet: 'The parts are tastefully arranged in a well-made walnut finished case with beige lined divisions and lock and key.' To add to their attraction, small parts were held in glass-topped boxes, and the gears and wheels were displayed on a peg board in a central partition. In 1909 the largest set still retained a sufficiently extensive number

THE WORLD'S MECHANICAL
WONDERS IN EVERY HOME

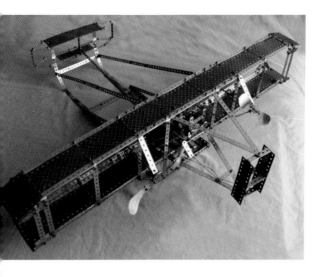

The Wright 'Flyer' model could be constructed from a No. 6 set, using instructions from a 1909 supplement. This model has later plates (blue) added, but in 1909 cardboard fillers would have been used. The model advertised Meccano in the 1910 Gamages catalogue.

No. 6 Meccano set in presentation cabinet, c. 1911–12. Most of the brass gears and wheels are stamped 'Patented 1911', to acknowledge Hornby's patent method of securing the bosses on to the wheel blanks.

parts to build large models, but by 1911 ̣ number of strips and girders in these ̣s was dramatically reduced, partly ̣mpensated for by the inclusion of the ̣w flanged plates, but permitting a ̣nificant reduction in prices.

For 1911, the year of the coronation ̣George V, Hornby produced a new ̣rter set priced at 3s. The 'Meccano ̣yal' outfit was contained in a very ̣ractive tin-printed box with raised ̣tering on the lid, enamelled in bright ̣l. The manual of instructions for the ̣yal' set, still subtitled 'Mechanics ̣de Easy', included fourteen simple ̣dels, most making use of the new (and ̣w ubiquitous) rectangular flanged plate ̣tained in the set.

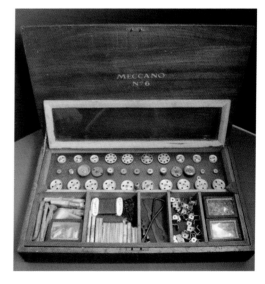

In 1912 or early 1913 an unusual single-purpose set was produced, to ̣ncide with the introduction of windmill sails (part no. 61). The 'Windmill' was a major departure at this time: designed to make just one model, the ̣fit was contained in a striking full-colour box. Only one surviving ̣mple of this set is known (see top of page 17).

In the five years from 1908 Meccano had become a product with ̣rldwide sales. Hornby had set up companies in France and Germany.

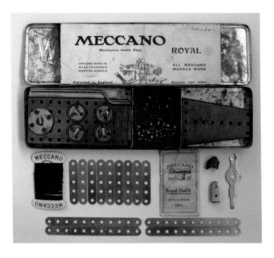

The 'Meccano Royal' set produced for the coronation year, 1911. It became the No. 0 set in 1913.

The 1911 book of instructions still includes the subtitle 'Mechanics Made Easy'.

He planned to establish agencies in the United States but was engaged in a patent battle with the American Model Builder company. To meet the growing demand for his product at home and abroad, he needed better manufacturing facilities. He had moved in 1909 from Duke Street to larger premises at a former carriage works in West Derby Road, Liverpool, but by 1913 his rapidly expanding business, including a significant level of export to the United States, and his plans for the future demanded new and larger premises. These were to be provided by building a new factory at Binns Road, Old Swan, within easy reach of Liverpool docks. The move took place in 1914 and the next two years to 1916 were to prove momentous for Meccano.

The First World War seems to have had little immediate impact on the home front. In the autumn of 1914 Meccano announced the 1914-15 model-building competition, which was to have far-reaching benefits for the development of the Meccano system. The first prize for the competition was £50, then a very large sum of money, equivalent to about a year's wages for a Binns Road employee. The ability of Frank Hornby to provide such prizes is a measure of the success of Meccano, even at this early time. Prize competitions made very good business sense: the competitions attracted new purchases, and the entries were a source of new models and ideas, which the competition rules made clear could be used by Meccano without any further payment to the entrants. As a result of the ten thousand entries to the competition, Meccano had a supply of models that began a transformation of the Meccano system and realised its potential for building complex mechanisms that accurately replicated real engineering.

Although it was awarded only a shared second prize in the competition, the model that captured

imagination of men and boys alike was the motor-car chassis by Frederick Gordon Crosby. It was the first realistic model of a motor-car chassis to appear in Meccano publications. Crosby was a draughtsman at the time but became an illustrator for *Autocar* magazine and is now well-known as a motoring artist and the creator of the Jaguar Cars mascot. Thirty years old in 1915, he confirms the accuracy of the advertising slogan used by Meccano: 'The best age to start Meccano is anywhere between 5 and 90.' The model also appeared in an article in the *Light Car* magazine in 1915 and was printed by Meccano as the first large-format model leaflet.

The unique 'Windmill' set, c. 1912–13 (see page 15).

The prize-winning models were published in book form and show how successful Meccano was worldwide, a considerable number of entries coming from the United States and France. Meccano operations in Germany had been suspended with the internment of the Berlin office manager, and so no models of German origin were included. The book includes advertising for a range of new Meccano parts and the first of a series of so-called 'Inventor's' outfits. These outfits provided a means of marketing new parts and initially included the book of prize models.

A short-lived range of Meccano outfits with an electric motor was also illustrated. These were intended primarily for the American market and used an electric motor manufactured by the American toy company Lionel.

The F. Gordon Crosby chassis featured in the 1914–15 book of prize models; this is a rebuild of the model by the author.

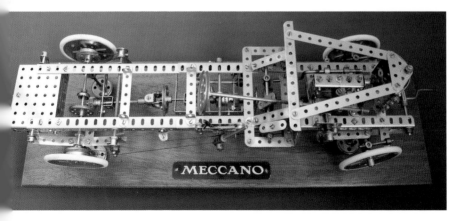

The Inventor's outfit included new parts to enhance the main outfits.

Below:
An example of the 1916 outfit 2X, the earliest set to include any form of motor. These sets, aimed at the American market, characteristically carry the slogan 'Engineering in miniature'.

The popularity Meccano had now grow to such an extent that was regarded as a toy occupy fathers and sons every station in socie Even men in positions authority, such as Winst Churchill, found Hornby's construction system enthralling.

A further competition in 1915– enabled a completely new instruction manu entitled *Book No. 1*, to be produced, contain many of the models from the competitio The two models that shared the first pr were given special prominence: a loom by Yoxall of Nelson, Lancashire, was the m sophisticated and complex model yet creat and a designing machine by William H. Ma of New York, called by Meccano ' 'Meccanograph'. Both models eventua resulted in specialised parts: shuttles a healds for the loom, and a designing table the Meccanograph. Hornby was so taken the designing machine that in late 1916 produced a special Meccanograph manu Thousands of boys have made this model

Winston Churchill, with his son Randolph and two nephews, building a Meccano model bridge in the winter of 1915–16. Painting by John Spencer Churchill.

...use themselves and their parents and, perhaps even more than the ...nous block-setting crane, it is still a favourite at Meccano clubs and ...hibitions.

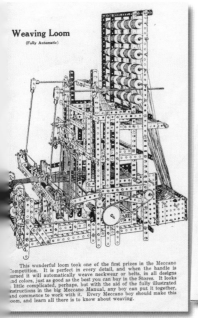

Weaving Loom
(Fully Automatic)

This wonderful loom took one of the first prizes in the Meccano Competition. It is perfect in every detail, and when the handle is ...urned it will automatically weave neckwear or belts, in all designs ...nd colors, just as good as the best you can buy in the Stores. It looks ... little complicated, perhaps, but with the aid of the fully illustrated ...instructions in the big Meccano Manual, any boy can put it together, ...and commence to work with it. Every Meccano boy should make this ...oom, and learn all there is to know about weaving.

The joint prize-winning models in the 1915–16 competition – a loom and the Meccanograph – both became popular models.

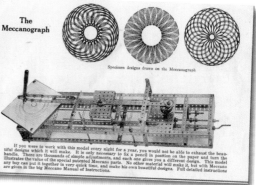

The Meccanograph

Specimen designs drawn on the Meccanograph

If you were to work with this model every night for a year, you would not be able to exhaust the beautiful designs which it will make. It is only necessary to fix a pencil in position on the paper and turn the handle. There are thousands of simple adjustments, and each one gives you a different design. This model illustrates the value of the special patented Meccano parts. No other material will make it, but with Meccano any boy can put it together in very quick time, and make his own beautiful designs. Full detailed instructions are given in the big Meccano Manual of Instructions.

THE NEW MECCANO

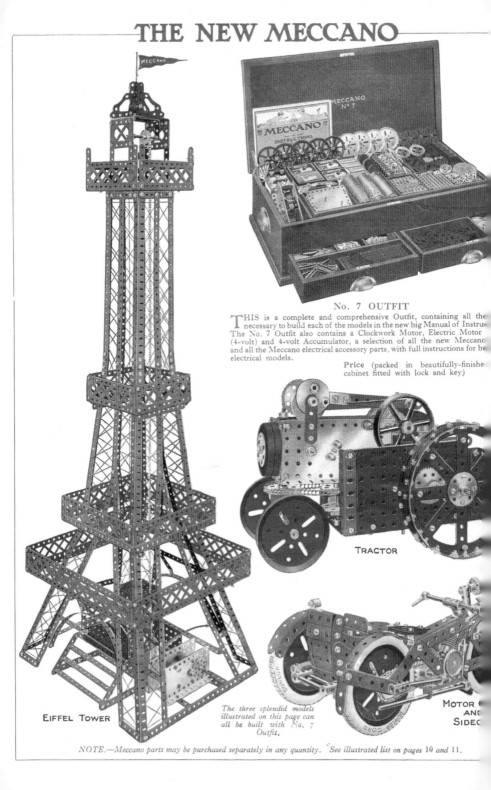

No. 7 OUTFIT

THIS is a complete and comprehensive Outfit, containing all the necessary to build each of the models in the new big Manual of Instru The No. 7 Outfit also contains a Clockwork Motor, Electric Motor (4-volt) and 4-volt Accumulator, a selection of all the new Meccano and all the Meccano electrical accessory parts, with full instructions for b electrical models.

Price (packed in beautifully-finishe cabinet fitted with lock and key)

TRACTOR

EIFFEL TOWER

The three splendid models illustrated on this page can all be built with No. 7 Outfit.

MOTOR C AND SIDEC

NOTE.—*Meccano parts may be purchased separately in any quantity. See illustrated list on pages 10 and 11.*

EXPANSION AND CONSOLIDATION: THE 1920s

WHEN THE First World War ended, Meccano production resumed unrestricted by wartime shortages, enabling an expansion of the range of Meccano products. By the end of 1920 a new wing of the Liverpool Binns Road factory was nearing completion to accommodate the production of the new Hornby clockwork trains. The company employed over 1,200 workers and could rightly claim that Meccano had become a popular indoor recreation for boys in every civilised country, appealing both to boys and their parents because of its excellent manufacture and presentation. The success of Meccano was largely due to Frank Hornby's business skill and his flair for presentation, but the interest in Meccano was also stimulated by sophisticated advertising, by the *Meccano Magazine*, which already had a large circulation (about forty thousand), and by the activities of the Meccano Guild, founded in 1919.

The first issue of the *Meccano Magazine* was produced in September 1916; initially it was given away through Meccano dealers. To begin with, correspondence from Meccano clubs and boys took up most of the magazine, but it was also an important medium for advertising new parts, manuals and kits. Frank Hornby wrote his 'Life Story of Meccano' for the magazine, and there were a few articles on new models. During 1921 Ellison Hawks, a well-known author of a wide range of popular science books, was appointed editor of the magazine and advertising manager for the company. Under his direction the magazine grew to encyclopaedic proportions, covering a wide range of topics, including engineering, hobbies such as stamp collecting, and stories of famous men from all walks of life. The magazine became an important source of ideas for models, providing monthly articles on the latest developments in engineering, and encouraging boys to experiment with their Meccano sets to create new and better models.

The development of Meccano from an educational toy to a popular hobby was also helped by the formation of local Meccano clubs. In 1918 correspondence with Meccano Ltd indicated that 'a new and vigorous movement was spreading throughout the country'. Boys were banding

Opposite:
The Eiffel Tower in the new colours and the magnificent No. 7 outfit in its cabinet, from a 1927 Meccano publicity booklet.

Meccano booklet giving advice to leaders worldwide on how to run a Meccano club.

HOW TO RUN A
MECCANO
CLUB

THE MECCANO GUILD
A WORLD WIDE FELLOWSHIP OF BOYS

Published by
MECCANO LIMITED
LIVERPOOL

Advertising for the much improved *Meccano Magazine* in the late 1920s.

THE
"MECCANO MAGAZINE"
A Fine Engineering Monthly for Boys

The *Meccano Magazine*, published in the interests of boys, contains splendid articles on such subjects as Railways, Famous Engineers and Inventors, Electricity, Bridges, Cranes, Wonderful Machinery, Aeroplanes, Latest Patents, Radio, Stamps, Photography and Books. New Meccano models and new parts are announced from time to time; special competitions are arranged for Meccano boys, and there are articles also for owners of Hornby Trains.

The *Meccano Magazine* is published on the 1st of each month, and has a circulation of over 60,000 copies per issue. It may be ordered from your Meccano dealer or if desired, it will be mailed direct by Meccano Ltd., Binns Road, Liverpool (post free) for six months 4/-, or twelve months 8/-. Send 6d. in stamps for a specimen copy, post free.

Price
6d.

PUBLISHED BY MECCANO LTD., BINNS ROAD, LIVERPOOL.

together to form Meccano clubs. Frank Hornby recognised the potential of these clubs and in 1918 he ran an essay competition in the *Meccano Magazine* on 'How I would run a Meccano club'.

The formation of the Meccano Guild was announced in September 1919. The principles on which the guild was founded had much in common with the Boy Scout movement, founded in 1908, encouraging good citizenship, and the development of skills for life. A personal message from Frank Hornby, who as President took a close interest in the guild, emphasised the fostering of 'clear mindedness, truthfulness, ambition, and initiative in boys'. The spirit of the clubs was motivated by a need for a society where every member played his part, and so boys were told in the President's address: 'You must first make up your mind that you are not joining for what you can get but for what you can give.' By 1932 the guild had a worldwide membership of over one hundred thousand.

In the early 1920s electrical technology was becoming commonplace. Many of the new houses being built for the middle classes were now wired for electricity. The electrical side of Meccano was spurred on by the development of an improved and home-produced electric motor in 1920, and the introduction of two electrical accessory outfits, called X1 and X2, which enabled boys to experiment with low-voltage applications to their models. A lead-acid accumulator provided the power source and was included in the X2 electrical outfit. An electrical outfit manual included a few models modified to use the electrical parts, but most were somewhat behind the times, such as a crane, and an early electric underground train.

The range of parts was continually being augmented, allowing more sophisticated models that better represented the engineering achievements of the 1920s. The introduction of bevel gears, architraves and girder frames

Left: An X1 electrical accessory outfit for the French market. Note the small-parts boxes labelled in English.

Middle: The same set for the English market.

Bottom: The X2 electrical outfit. The crane is operated by the 1921 electric motor powered by the now rare accumulator.

pported the production of a further Inventor's outfit, d so the original set was renamed 'Inventor's A' and e new one was called the 'Inventor's B' outfit.

The extensive and well-presented No. 7 outfit troduced in 1922, and contained in a very well-made binet, included most of the new parts. However, tle use was made of these parts in the instruction

The Inventor's B set used to promote new parts introduced in 1918. Note the colourful picture on the box.

The Meccano No. 7 'Superset' of 1926 was coveted by many a boy and is now the pinnacle of aspiration for the Meccano collector.

manual models beyond merely using an electric motor to drive models. Neither was the dramatic increase in the size of the largest set, with the addition of longer angle girders (18½ and 24½ inches), plus many other parts accompanied by an extensive range of new and larger models. Most models in the instruction manual had previously been published and most are quite uninspiring, but among them are three celebrated models that were published as special large-format instruction leaflets: the motor chassis, the loom, and the high speed ship's coaler.

In 1923 Meccano Ltd was fortunate to recruit an enterprising young Meccano enthusiast who had a major impact on the development of the *Meccano Magazine* and Meccano modelling. Hubert Lansley joined Meccano after his own magazine, entitled *Meccano Engineer*, came to the notice of Ellison Hawks. After being ticked off for using the Meccano name without permission, Lansley was quickly recruited to assist in the Binns Road advertising department. In his own words:

I was given a short, terse briefing [by Ellison Hawks]. I was to carve out a space for myself at the far end of the advertising department and there build models and supply as much copy as I could for the *Meccano Magazine*.

Lansley's modelling skills were put to good use. He saw the potential of the No. 7 set to create a range of more realistic and up-to-date models. One of his earlier models to appear was the motorcycle and sidecar based on his own BSA V-twin 980cc combination, (see page 20) first published in January 1926 in the *Meccano Magazine*, which states that the model 'should prove to be no light tax on the ingenuity of even less experienced Meccano Boys', but the realistic appearance

f the model repays the painful application of nimble fingers. The full versatility
nd potential of the No. 7 set was realised with the publication in 1928 of a
eries of 'Supermodel' leaflets largely as a result of Hubert Lansley's work.

Meccano was now well established as a means of building and testing
rototypes of real projects. One of Hubert Lansley's first assignments was
o cover the British Empire Exhibition at Wembley in 1924, where one of
ne exhibitors was George Constantinesco, a well-known inventor and
ngineer, who had previously been interviewed for the *Meccano Magazine*
bout the use of Meccano in his research and experimental work.
onstantinesco had patented over 130 inventions and, most notably, had
nvented the system for synchronising the firing of machine guns through
ne revolving propellers of fighter aircraft in the First World War. Recorded
ses of Meccano include designs for a lifting device for the Mersey Docks
nd a bridge in New York Harbour.

The success of Meccano is manifest in the thousands of boys who, through their interest in building things that really worked, developed an understanding of the principles of engineering and subsequently became successful professional engineers. Edgar Whately (1913–90) was typical of these. From the age of fourteen until he was eighteen, he enthusiastically entered Meccano competitions by sending photographs of his models to Meccano Ltd. Although he did not win a major prize, he was a frequent runner-up and in total won prizes in twelve competitions between 1927 and 1931.

Whately left school at sixteen, with his school certificates describing a talented boy, particularly in draughtsmanship and craft. In 1929 he joined Ferranti Ltd, where he stayed for forty-eight years, in various electrical engineering and design positions, retiring in 1977 as a Senior Design Engineer. His main work was related to aircraft equipment, particularly artificial horizons (attitude indicators) and gyro-stabilisation devices, in both of which

fields Ferranti was pre-eminent during the Second World War and the later 1940s and 1950s. During the war he was also associated with work on proximity fuses (for anti-aircraft guns) and radar. Typically for his age group, he continued to study at night school into the 1940s, eventually becoming a Chartered Electrical Engineer. He attributed his success as an engineer to his early interest in Meccano.

Consolation prize awarded to Edgar Whately in a Meccano model-building competitions. The wallet is inscribed 'With the compliments of Frank Hornby'. As well as competition prizes, wallets like this may also have been used as complimentary items for sales representatives or special gifts from Frank Hornby to Meccano workers.

The traction engine Supermodel, designed by Hubert Lansley using parts introduced in 1928, was capable of hauling his colleague from the model room.

When finished, the Meccano Traction Engine will haul its builder along.

Although the range of outfits from No. 00 to No. 7, with associated accessory outfits, remained constant from 1922 until 1934, the contents of the outfits changed nearly every year and in 1926 a major presentational change was made with the introduction of the 'New Meccano' in colour.

The new, coloured Meccano provided for much-improved advertising, which, under the direction of Ellison Hawks, significantly contributed to increasing sales. Catalogues of products had been produced from as early as 1916 but these had lacked the dramatic use of colour. Well-designed leaflets of 1926 and 1927 strongly promoted the 'New Meccano', using existing models with parts suitably coloured in.

Publicity booklet from 1927 showing the 'New Meccano' parts in red and green.

The two years of 1926 and 1927 seem to have been a period of confusion regarding presentation. The 'New Meccano' had been heralded as the introduction of striking colour for a few parts, leaving strips and girders nickel plated. Most of the coloured parts were confined to the larger sets. It seems a decision was made in the first half of 1927 to produce nearly all Meccano parts in colour. The light-red and pea-green shades were soon replaced by a much darker Burgundy red and bottle green, and the layout of the sets was also changed.

The No. 5 set sold particularly well, having a comprehensive range of parts, and enabling the building of a good range of models. It would have cost £2 15s in 1926 and so was within the reach of middle-class parents who wanted their sons to do well in the new world of engineering. Even if the luxury No. 7 set could not be afforded outright at £18 10s, it was always possible to add to the No. 5 with accessory sets, the 5a costing a further 10s. (The average weekly wage in 1926 was about £2.) However, like the No. 7 set, the 6a, converting a No. 6 set into the No. 7, was still within the reach of only the wealthy at £10 10s.

Despite the success of the larger sets, Meccano did not neglect the market for smaller, less expensive lines. The quality of the smallest sets, Nos. 00 and 0, was equal to that of the large sets in both packaging and contents.

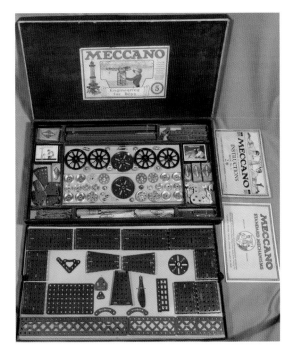

Right: Two No. 5 sets from 1927 (top) and 1928, showing the changes in colour layout.

As well as being a medium that could be applied to the development of technological research, Meccano has always enabled more whimsical creation limited only by the imagination. Competition entries encouraged imaginative boys to provide models representing people, animals and simple toys. These 'simplicity' models, which were included in the instructions for smaller sets gave a suitable introduction for younger boys and girls to the joys of Meccano. Smaller sets were also promoted by an amusing advertising booklet, *Adventure in Meccanoland*, produced by Hubert Lansley in 1925. The booklet tells a fair story about 'Dick' (who frequently appears in Meccano advertising booklets who, on being given his first Meccano set, falls asleep and dreams of a land populated by Meccanitians – people made out of Meccano parts. All but two of the models illustrated in the booklet could be built with a No. 1 outfit. The booklet was produced in many languages, including Chinese.

By the end of the 1920s motor-car ownership was within the reach of most middle-class families, who remained the main market for Meccano. 1927 Hubert Lansley, writing under the pseudonym of Edgar Wright

The No. 00 set was one of the smallest sets from 1928–9.

roduced a series of *Meccano Magazine* articles describing he reproduction of motor-car mechanics in Meccano. These led to he publication of a much-improved esign for the Meccano motor-car hassis. This model included ccurate Ackerman steering, a hree-speed and reverse gearbox hat really worked, and a working ifferential using the recently troduced bevel gears. The motor-r chassis proved to be a very opular model, being used both a shop display model r Meccano dealers and also as demonstration model in the lucation of motor mechanics.

Throughout the 1920s, despite e difficult economic times and hemployment of over one million, e sales of Meccano grew nificantly, sustained by the iddle-class market. According Hubert Lansley, who was sponsible for conducting factory urs, in the early 1920s the eccano factory assembled and cked some 8,500 sets each day, a figure that increased considerably by 30. In 1928 Meccano Ltd achieved a profit of £58,000, the highest level ained before the Second World War.

Adventures in Meccanoland, a story illustrated by amusing models that could be built with the No. 1 outfit.

The last years of the decade were also peak years for the introduction of w parts. In 1928 a further 'special' Inventor's accessory outfit was produced a way of selling new parts to boys who already had Meccano sets. However, s set failed to attract wide interest, despite the inclusion of some now highly ught-after parts, and was produced for only two years.

The most celebrated of the Supermodels, the giant block-setting crane, ich featured for many years on the cover of the instruction manuals, was st published in a leaflet in 1928. This model, subtitled 'The largest Meccano del', has come to represent the peak of Meccano modelling. Although it n be criticised for not using totally correct engineering, it provides a listic miniature of the harbour-building cranes that were widely used from

The redesigned 1927 motor-car chassis built by the author from instructions in the 1927 manual.

The rare special Inventor's outfit, produced from 1929 to market the range of newly introduced parts.

the early 1900s and, when built well, fully reproduces the movements of t_ real thing. *The Meccano Book of Engineerir* produced as a companion to the popu! *Hornby Book of Trains*, describes the cra in some detail.

To enhance the model of the bloc setting crane, the geared roller beari (GRB; part no. 167), perhaps the me desirable single Meccano part, w introduced in 1928. Although giver single part number, the bearing consi of two dished plates approximately inches in diameter and each with 1 teeth, one ring frame 10 inches diameter, sixteen ¾-inch flanged whe and pivot bolts, a 9½-inch strip, two bu wheels, and a 1½-inch axle. These we packaged in a well-made box with

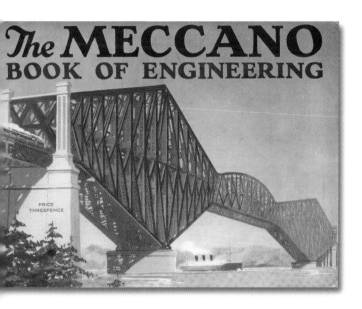

Left: *The Meccano Book of Engineering* describes recent achievements in civil engineering and the block-setting cranes used in the construction of harbours.

Below: The 1929 *Meccano Book of New Models* with the giant block-setting crane shown in real life and as a Meccano model. Six books of new models were published between 1928 and 1933.

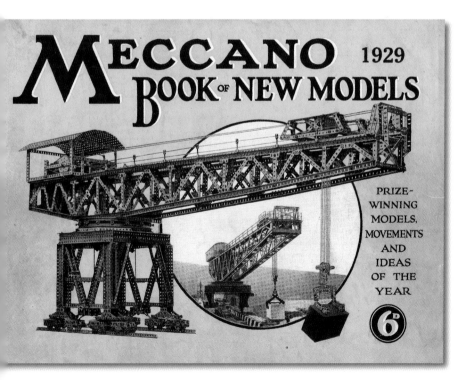

31

special sixteen-tooth pinion. The geared roller bearing appeared in sever colour schemes from 1928 to 1941.

Throughout the 1920s several improvements were made to the Meccan electric motor, making it both more convenient to operate and mo powerful. The motors, initially rated at 4 volts, later increased to 6 volt could still be powered by an accumulator but could now use a transforme from the mains electricity. This design of electric motor, eventually rated 20 volts from the mid-1930s, continued to be produced until the late 1960 In 1926 a much more powerful version was introduced in the United State powered directly from the 110-volt mains. The design was subsequent copied and produced in the United Kingdom, but still rated at 110 volts, requiring a lamp to reduce the voltage from 240 volts. Produced primari to power shop-display models, this potentially lethal motor, with exterr brushes and little protection for prying fingers, was also incorporated in some of the Supermodels.

For those without access to electricity, two alternative sources of pow were available. Before the First World War Hornby had imported a stea engine from a German manufacturer (possibly Märklin or Bing), which reproduced in 1920. At £1 7s 6d, this was a very expensive item, and so t much cheaper alternatives from continental manufacturers proved mo popular. A much more successful Meccano steam engine was introduced 1929, and sold for £1 1s. With well-made steam fittings and a vertical stea boiler with a nicely detailed outer boiler jacket, it was capable of drivi Meccano models such as the realistic steam excavator produced as a spec Supermodel.

The realistic steam excavator Supermodel, driven by the 1929 steam engine and one of the few models to make use of the digger bucket.

For those of lesser means, well-built clockwork motors (also initially of German origin) could be obtained as a No. 1, for 5s, and from 1931 as the more powerful No. 2, for 10s, both of the same robust design.

Throughout the 1920s the Meccano system had been significantly extended, incorporating new parts and giving more realism to better-designed models. Meccano had established itself clearly as the market leader and was recognised worldwide as a high-quality product. Frank Hornby had succeeded in his ambition to give every boy the opportunity to own a Meccano set, providing for every pocket with both large and small sets, and the facility to extend one's set from the smallest 00 set to the largest No. 7.

A shop-window display showing the range of products available from 1928 to the mid-1930s. The background is an original display card depicting the famous Supermodels. The geared roller bearing and 1929 steam engine can also be seen in the display.

MECCANO
OUTFIT "L"

Meccano Motor Chassis

MECCANO
INSTRUCTIONS

MECCANO
CLOCKWORK MOTOR No.1

MECCANO
ELECTRIC MOTOR No. E6

MECCANO
ELECTRIC MO
No. E6

MECCANO
PARTS AND
HOW TO USE
COPYRIGHT BY MECCANO (LIVERPOOL)
BINNS ROAD, LIVERPOOL 13, ENGLAND

MECCANO
INSTRUCTIONS FOR OUTFITS F–L
PAGE 1/9

COPYRIGHT BY MECCANO LTD., BINNS ROAD, LIVERPOOL 13.

MECCAN
STANDARD
MECHANISMS

THE GOLDEN AGE:
THE 1930s

THE DEPRESSION of the early 1930s provided challenges to Meccano that resulted in a general reduction in the size and prices of the largest sets. owever, the 1930s were a golden age of innovation for the now well-tablished Meccano company. To respond to competition, especially from e resurgent German toymakers Märklin, and to address falling sales of eccano construction sets, new ranges of constructional toys were croduced. The first of these were the Aeroplane Constructor sets of 1931.

The first Aeroplane Constructor sets were rather drab in appearance, ing produced in a dull silver-grey finish with flat wing profiles, and based First World War biplanes such as the Sopwith Camel (shown on the box el). These sets were largely compatible with standard Meccano, having e same hole spacing and bolt size, but included a completely new range parts.

In late 1932 an improved range of aero parts was introduced; better-ofiled wings with curved edges, engine nacelles, wheel shields (spats) the undercarriage and improved landing wheels gave a marked increase realism.

Aeroplanes were now commonplace, and the technology of flight had eloped significantly since the pioneering days of the Wright brothers. In y 1930 the public imagination had been captured by the achievements of y Johnson, who, at the age of twenty-seven, had completed a solo flight 11,000 miles from London to Australia in a second-hand De Havilland sy Moth biplane. This biplane was modelled by Meccano; a simpler structional item than the larger aeroplane sets, it was produced as the s. 0 and 00 sets in an extensive range of colours and various packaging m 1932 to 1941.

Aeroplane Constructor sets were very popular, and Meccano provided nge of export lines for the Continent with appropriate national markings improved wing shapes. Despite the models' inability to fly, some boys vitably attempted to propel them through the air – with disastrous sequences. While the models themselves did little to develop an

Opposite:
The magnificent
'L' set, introduced
in 1934 with the
new instruction
manuals and
supermodel leaflet
for the motor
chassis based
on the Bentley
sports saloon.

Above left:
An early Meccano
No. I aeroplane
constructor set,
showing the flat
wing profile and
dull paint finish.

Above right:
A No.I aeroplane
outfit in its original
box (with military
markings), and
a biplane
constructed with
the alternative
civil markings
(introduced in
1938).

understanding of the principles of flight, the instructions for building the
included a clear description of how to fly an aeroplane and of t
fundamentals of aerodynamics, which probably encouraged many boys
take up flying careers, and later, in wartime, to join the RAF.

Building on the success of these new products, a splendid new range
'special' Aeroplane Constructor sets was introduced in time for Christm
1933.

The largest of these sets, the No. 2S, was contained in a box measuri
60 cm by 50 cm and included new and superior parts for constructing aircr
with a more up-to-date appearance. The extensive range of parts was stru

Meccano No. 00
aeroplane set
with constructed
examples in late
wartime colours.

nto card, an operation that emanded concentration and atience, resulting in an ye-catching display that ould have delighted many a hild on Christmas morning. omparatively expensive at 1 5s, and comparable in rice to a mid-range standard eccano set, these sets nabled forty-four different roplanes to be constructed.

well-produced manual r the sets used evocative notographic images of the odels in simulated flight and ncluded several pages on vanced flying techniques, including aerobatics. These special aeroplane tfits are among the finest toys to be produced by any British manufacturer.

Late 1930s French aero constructor set No. 1S showing the better-shaped wings used in continental and export sets.

The comprehensive No. 2S special aero constructor set, c. 1938, with civil marking, and two examples of planes built from the set.

Right: The 1933
No. 2 Motor Car
Constructor outfit
and the special
lighting set
designed for it.

Below: Motor
Car Constructor
advertising poster
from 1935 showing
the range of
colours; the car
on the left is a
non-Constructor
car introduced in
1936 and modelled
on the MG sports
car.

Of equally high quality and no less innovative were the Motor Car Constructor sets produced in time for Christmas 1932. Available in a range of striking colour combinations, these outfits were beautifully made and presented. Parts in the outfit were pressed from thinner-gauge steel than standard Meccano parts and bolted together using nickel-plated 6BA nuts and bolts, as used in the No. 0 aeroplane sets. The outfits were therefore totally incompatible with standard Meccano. Priced at £1 5s, this was a quality product with a well-designed clockwork motor that gave a run of 50 feet to a wide range of thirty-two different cars, including boat-tailed racing cars similar to those seen on the Brooklands motor-racing circuit. Assembling the cars is quite difficult, requiring careful alignment of the parts and close attention to the rather brief instructions leaflet. In the first sets dummy headlights were fitted, but in 1933 the range of sets was revised and a special lighting outfit was introduced to enable headlights to be operated from the dashboard, powered by a 4-volt flat battery.

With the introduction of the smaller and less expensive No. 1 Motor Car outfit in 1933, the original outfit was designated the No. 2, with the addition of a diecast driver, and a spare-wheel cover instead of a fifth road wheel. The No. 1 outfit, priced at 14s 6d, was equally well produced, also fitted with a clockwork motor, but totally incompatible with the No. 2 outfit, except for using the same 6BA nuts and bolts. Although having fewer parts, the No. 1 car was in many ways even more tricky to assemble than the

A No. 1 Motor Car outfit in its original box with one of the models that could be constructed with the contents.

No. 2. Its smaller scale made it more awkward to manipulate, and alignmen of the parts more difficult. It lacked some of the alternative parts of the No 2 but still allowed construction of a good range of different cars, includin two- and four-seat open-top sports cars, a boat-tailed two-seat racing ca and a saloon with a choice of two different doors.

By the early 1930s, despite the recession, which did not affect all section of British society equally, the British toy trade was booming. The idea construction sets had caught the imagination not only of the public but als of manufacturers at home and abroad. A cheap alternative to Meccano, Tri was sold through retailers such as F. W. Woolworth at bargain prices as lo as 6d, and, although limited in the range of parts, Trix was a very good selle Meccano recognised the threat to its premier product and introduced the 'X series sets in time for Christmas 1932. Considered today to have bee something of an aberration, the 'X' series was an almost direct copy of Tr but, where Trix used 4BA bolts with the holes in the strips set diagonall Meccano 'X' series parts used standard Meccano bolts and wider strips wi parallel rows of holes spaced ¼ inch apart.

Meccano 'X' series outfits 1 and 2, with a model powered by the 'X' series clockwork motor.

A new, inexpensive clockwork motor was introduced for use with the ' series sets. Originally painted on one side in red and the other in green, wi a fixed key, the motor was subsequently modified and survived into the 197

s the 'Meccano Magic Motor'. Although the parts were compatible with standard Meccano, the sets could not overcome the strongly established competition, and so the 'X' series was withdrawn in 1936, with surplus parts being sold at a reduced price repackaged as 'The British Model Builder'.

In 1933, as part of the continuing diversification of the product range, Meccano departed from its traditional constructional sets and introduced a new range of attractive science-experiment sets. Meccano's competitors, such as Kay, Lotts and BGL (British Games Ltd), were regularly advertising chemistry and electrical experiment sets in the *Meccano Magazine*. Although not strictly construction sets, the Meccano Elektron and Kemex sets were strongly educational and well placed to exploit the potential market created by the growing interest in educating the young about the sciences of electricity and chemistry. These sets are among the most attractive and well-presented of Meccano products; eye-catching use of colour, well-designed layouts and well-made parts immediately give an impression of quality. What boy, or his father, could resist the array of interesting new pieces with a high-minded educational purpose?

The instruction booklets for both Elektron and Kemex sets were very well produced, with attractive front covers. The combined Kemex manual for the Nos. 2 and 3 sets has forty-nine pages of well-written descriptions of

A 1935 No. 2 Elektron outfit, showing the shocking coil and lamp made with the parts included.

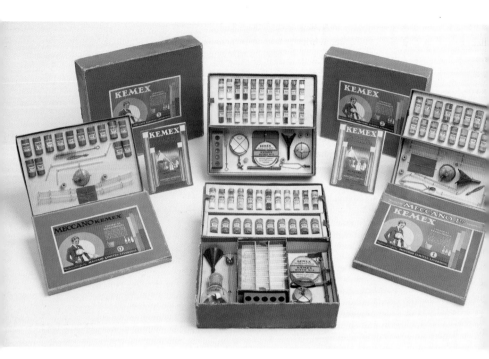

Above:
Attractively
presented Kemex
outfits Nos. 0, 1, 2
and 3, produced
from 1933 to
1940.

Opposite, top:
Meccano A set:
initially the
smallest set in the
1934–5 range of
sets in the new
colour scheme.

Opposite
bottom: The
comprehensive
range of parts
available in the
mid-1930s

experiments with well-thought-out explanations, providing clear instructic
in the basics of chemistry. These booklets would even today provide a ver
sound basis for a good GCSE in science and are a further example of the hig
quality of Meccano products. However, the sets were to have a short span o
production, being withdrawn from sale by 1941, and the small number o
sets now found indicates that they were not as popular as other products o
the period, such as the Motor Car and Aeroplane Constructor sets.

The early 1930s had been a period of development and innovation in th
Meccano product range. However, apart from the introduction of new par
and coloured Meccano in 1926, Meccano standard construction sets ha
changed little since 1916. By 1934 Meccano sales had declined dramaticall
to less than half the level of 1930. At the end of 1934, in time for Christma
major changes were announced: a new colour scheme – gold for strips an
girders, and blue with a yellow cross-hatched pattern for plates – replace
the well-established red and green scheme; the contents of the sets, no
identified by letters A–L rather than numbers, were significantly change
with no simple relationship between the old numbered sets and the ne
lettered sets; the packaging also changed from the rather dull black carto
to bright red boxes showing two or three well-dressed boys building th
block-setting crane in the new colours.

There are some indications that this change was too hurried, because, while announcing 'New colours, new parts and new manuals', the manuals contained exactly the same models, merely retouched to represent the new colours. Furthermore, just three years later another major overhaul of the system took place with the reintroduction of numbered sets, this time from 0 to 10, again with completely revised contents, but now accompanied by new manuals with many new and improved models. Accompanying both these changes were transitional sets that could be bought to convert numbered sets to lettered sets and later, in 1937–8, vice-versa. These connecting outfits are now rare items in any condition. In many ways 1934–7 was a transitional period, reflecting the turmoil in the world

An accessory outfit, named 'Da', converting set D into set E.

economy and the unstable political situation in Europe. By 1938 sales of Meccano sets had again increased in Britain (nearly 50 per cent more than in 1934), but overseas sales continued to decline.

Throughout this period the range of standard Meccano parts remained substantially constant, with surprisingly few introductions to support the new range of sets. Flexible plates, introduced for the first time, initially in fibre-board, improved the appearance of large models. The range of parts available included gears to give ratios of 1:1, 2:1, 3:1, 5:1 and 7:1; and the use of spur gears and worm gear, and of sprockets with fourteen, eighteen, twenty-eight, thirty-six and fifty-six teeth linked by chain, gave Meccano enormous potential that went far beyond a mere toy. These spur, bevel (right-angle) and helical (spiral) gears enable differential and epicyclic gear trains to be included in clocks and orreries, resulting in a very high level of accuracy.

While the large number of special parts now provided offered the modeller opportunity for great realism, many were not included in the contents of the standard outfits and had to be purchased separately, even when the largest set, L, costing £20 10s, was bought.

The L set, with its vast range of parts, gave immense scope for building complex and realistic Meccano models. Included in the set were twenty-three of the forty-two different Supermodel leaflets then available. Some of the leaflets were modified to represent the new colour scheme, but most were simply reprinted with little change. The only completely new Supermodel leaflet specifically produced for the L set was a revised Meccano motor chassis based on the 3.5-litre Bentley introduced in 1933 and promoted as the 'silent sports car'. The Meccano model (see contents page ccurately reproduces the chassis layout, including working brakes, suspension, steering and a four-speed and reverse gearbox, but the instructions are complex and difficult to follow, and the all-pinion gearbox with its sloppy gear change was very unreliable. It was certainly not a project for any but the most intelligent and dexterous of boys.

The year 1936 marked the end of an era for both Meccano and the nation with the death of both Frank Hornby and King George V. In September 1936 Frank Hornby underwent an operation for a heart condition but survived for only three days, dying on 21 September, five years to the day after he was first elected as MP for the Everton ward of Liverpool. Although Hornby had retained the title of Managing Director of Meccano Ltd, from the late 1920s the running of the business was mainly in the hands of a number of long-serving aides. Hornby's reduced involvement was a consequence of his declining health and his interest in politics. Over a quarter of a century he had transformed the production of a toy devised to amuse his children into an international business producing a wide range of quality toys with annual

Left: No. 0, the smallest set in the new range of sets 0–10 in 1937.

sales of £5 million. Although the company was taken over by his son Roland, some of the inventiveness, vision and dedication to creating a world of 'Meccano boys' that drove his father was missing.

Following the abdication crisis of 1936, Britain looked forward to a new era with the coronation of George VI in 1937. The marketing of Meccano sets also entered a new era with the reintroduction of numbered sets. Announced in October 1937, the new range of sets retained the expensive gold and blue colour scheme, but was accompanied by a completely new range of manuals and represented many improvements over the letter series outfits. Reducing the contents of the largest set, No. 10, enabled it to be sold for a much lower price, £11 11s, little more than half the price of the massive L set, which cost over £20.

The new range of sets included an increased number of flexible plates and a more balanced range of girders and strips, enabling the building of impressive models such as a giant liner, over 6 feet in length and looking very much like the *Queen Mary*, then the world's largest liner, and the

The versatile No. 10 outfit introduced in late 1937, with new manuals describing a completely new range of models.

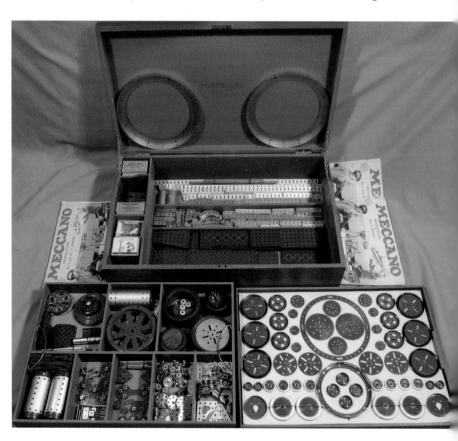

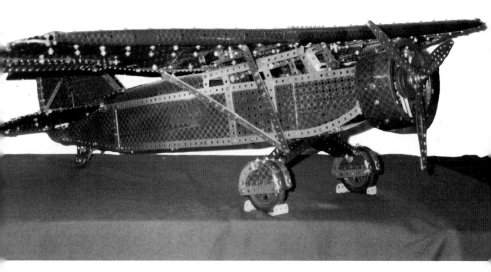

ell-proportioned cabin monoplane. Also with a sufficient complement of ars to enable the building of motor vehicles with working clutch, gearboxes d brakes, the No. 10 set provided the versatility and economy to remain e flagship set for the next forty years.

The new range of sets was marketed only from Christmas 1937 until 1940, en the Second World War intervened. Between 1939 and 1941 a short-lived nge of military-themed toys was produced. The Mechanised Army outfit, roduced in 1939, was the last new pre-war Meccano outfit. Fully compatible th standard Meccano but painted in 'army green', the parts in this outfit parted from the normal, having fewer holes in plates and wheels. The No. 0 roplanes were given a wartime livery and produced in camouflage colours service grey and sold in smaller wartime-packaged boxes. Plans were made 1940 for a whole range of army outfits but these were never marketed. spite paper shortages, Meccano instruction manuals continued to be oduced until 1941, with some changes to the models in the Nos. 9 and 10 nuals. The models were still shown with yellow cross-hatching on the plates an insert stated that this had been discontinued, giving rise to speculation t another revision of the colour scheme was planned.

From 1 January 1942 the production of metal toys was prohibited by ernment order and the Meccano factory was given over completely to war rk – making frames for Wellington bombers, bomb-release mechanisms, odermic needles, and fuses. A wartime poster for National Savings, created om Purvis, shows an idealised boy remembering more peaceful times while structing a railway breakdown crane. Meccano was now part of the national ture of Britain.

A model built by the author from parts in the 1938 No. 10 outfit: the cabin monoplane (model 10.10) remodelled as a Lysander spotter aircraft of the Second World War.

Left: An accessory outfit for the revised range of sets converting a set No. 6 into a set No. 7.

Below: The short-lived Mechanise Army outfit of 1939, showing the plates with fewer than standard perforations.

Opposite page: The 1941 National Savings poster by Tom Purvis – Meccano had become a familiar pastime.

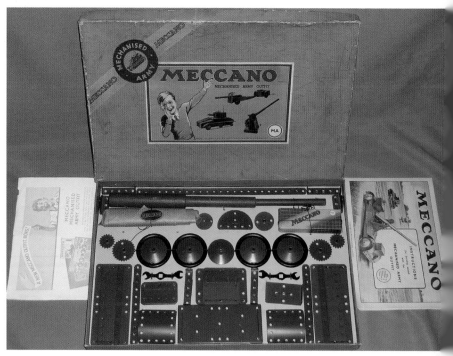

LEND TO DEFEND HIS RIGHT TO BE FREE

BUY NATIONAL SAVINGS CERTIFICATES

VOL. XXXIX No. 12   DECEMBER 195

MECCANO
MAGAZINE

THE JOYS OF CHRISTMAS

POST-WAR
REGENERATION: 1945–64

A FTER THE WAR the return to full production was slow, partly because of the restrictions on supplies of raw materials, but also because some of the factory's press tools had been scrapped to make way for war work. The factory concentrated its efforts on restoring the production of the standard Meccano sets, but it was not until Christmas 1950 that the full range of sets was again available. Even then, the range of parts had been rationalised and more than fifty pre-war parts were declared obsolete. The Meccano Aeroplane and Motor Car Constructor outfits were never to reappear; the pre-war prototypes on which these were modelled were now old-fashioned, new designs and press tools would be needed, and tinplate toys were already being overtaken by diecast products. Meccano Ltd would also concentrate resources on developing the popular ranges of Dinky Toys and Hornby Dublo trains introduced before the war.

In late 1945 a notice advised Meccano dealers of the limited availability Meccano sets but promised that outfits 0, 1, 2 and 3 would be ready first, with parts beautifully enamelled in red and green'. The pre-war livery of blue and gold was quietly dropped, although production in these colours continued in France until the 1970s. The contents and packaging of these early post-war sets remained very much the same as the pre-war equivalents. To overcome continued printing shortages, box labels were modified and reduced in size, and manuals were reprints of pre-war editions. Manual covers reverted to the design of the accessory outfit manuals, printed in green for main outfits and orange for accessory sets.

With the reintroduction of the No. 9 set in 1948, new instruction manuals were published for all outfits from 0 to 9 and for some accessory outfits. The main outfit manuals carried a new and evocative cover illustration commissioned from the commercial artist W. H. Pinyon. The cover depicts two modern boys completing the now familiar block-setting crane recoloured in red and green, and watched over approvingly by their pipe-smoking father. Most of the revised manuals included only the existing models from the pre-war manuals and, although some models were updated, most were somewhat

Opposite:
A shop window
display of Meccano
products being
admired by
schoolboys: the
Meccano Magazine
cover for
December 1954.

51

Above: An early
post-war No. 1
outfit shown with
the 'utility' manual
necessitated by
printing
restrictions.

old-fashioned. The revisions to the No. 9 se
manual were more extensive, with new model
making good use of the parts in the outfit.

The No. 10 set was reintroduced fo
Christmas 1949, with some significant change
in the contents; clockwork and electric motor
included in the pre-war No. 10 outfit wer
deleted. However, there were increases in som
useful building parts, including additional lon
girders, large circular parts and more gears. Thes
changes resulted in a more balanced set an
increased the versatility for model building. Th
No. 10 manual, now separate from the No. 9, w
a reprint of the pre-war manual, with no ne
models, and with simple retouching to remo
the cross-hatching on the plates. The new cove
showing the pre-war giant block-setting cran
was a cause of much frustration to many, wh
realised that a similar crane could not be bu
even with this, the largest set. A further cause
disappointment was the back cover of the ne
manuals, which tantalisingly depicted Mecca
parts that had been available in 1940. In real
the range and availability of spare parts throu
high-street Meccano dealers was very limited a
never regained the pre-war levels.

Taking account of the reduced purchasi
power of the pound sterling, the reintroduced No. 10 set was good val
at just under £29, compared to the price of £30 in 1941. The oak-stain
beech presentation cabinet was particularly well made, with two lift-
trays containing all the parts, still strung, meticulously but laboriou:
onto yellow card.

By 1950 Meccano production had been steadily re-established; the
range of outfits, including accessory outfits and a useful new 'Gears Ou
A', were available. There were also promising plans to reintroduce some
the special parts still illustrated in the manuals. For the next two years furt
development would be restricted by the Korean War, which resulted
shortages of brass, nickel and steel. Meccano entered a 'black period' dur
1951 and 1952, when some parts were chemically blackened steel or
instead of brass-plated.

The first major post-war competition promoting Meccano
announced in October 1952. This was the first international competit

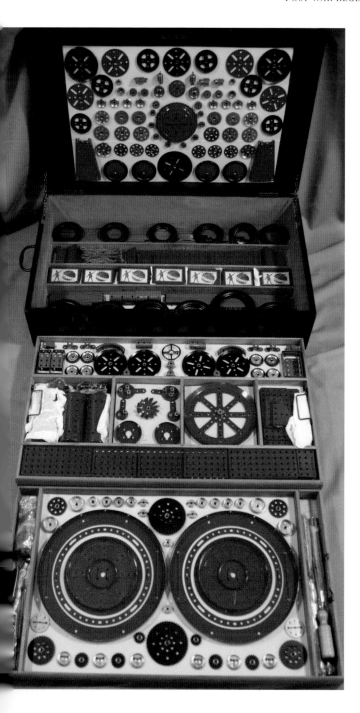

Above: Spare parts from the 1950s.

Left: The reintroduced post-war No. 10 set in the new colours of red and green, contained in a well-made oak-finished cabinet.

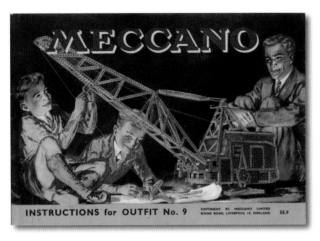

INSTRUCTIONS for OUTFIT No. 9

Above: The new cover for the revised manuals of 1954; the boys are the same but their father no longer smokes, as in the previous version shown on page 6.

since 1932 to offer substantia first prizes: £30 (more than the cost of a No. 10 set) for boys under ten years old, and £50 for those over ten years.

Announcing the winner of the competition in September 1953, the *Meccan Magazine*'s 'Spanner' (Norman Tudor) commented on the marked differences i the type of subject entere for this competition i contrast to 1932. In th earlier contest most of th principal prizes were awarded for cranes, ships and vehicles, whereas i 1953 'the larger prizes were earned by models of industrial machines an road making equipment with more originality in the entries generally That Meccano appealed to 'boys' of all ages was evident from the wid range of entrants to the competition: the oldest was eighty-two years ol and the youngest under three. Many entries in the over-sixteen categor were from considerably older enthusiasts, indicating that Meccano w becoming more established as an adu hobby. The entries for this and oth competitions increased the stock models for a new range of manuals a much-needed new models for the N 10 outfit.

A new set of instruction manuals a changes to the presentation of the outf came in 1954. A new model of a walki dragline was shown on the cover standard manuals, and a railw breakdown crane on accessory manua No plans were published for either these models. A small range of new pa was added to the contents of the larg outfits, including useful triangu flexible plates, and flexible plates w given slotted (instead of round) e holes, increasing the capacity to fabric streamlined models.

Main outfit cartons now had larger labels depicting the block-setting crane being built by two more modern-looking boys – though still in short trousers. Use of the giant block-setting crane indicated the outfit was a complete set. Virtually no other changes were made to the cartons, and parts were still attractively strung onto yellow card.

Models in these new manuals are not only more up to date but also much better representations of real vehicles and machines. They represent the highest level of realism achieved by Meccano in standard manuals and, many decades later, still attract interest and admiration today.

A completely new set of model plans for the No. 10 outfit replaced the revamped pre-war instructions, which by 1955 were very outmoded. These twenty special model leaflets represent the pinnacle of post-war Meccano modelling produced by Meccano Ltd. Initially only twelve leaflets were available and provided with the outfit. Unlike the Supermodel leaflets of the 1920s, these plans were designed specifically for the No. 10 outfit and so are generally of the same standard, making good use of the range of parts in the outfit.

The No. 10 outfit had now reached a stable state and would remain virtually unchanged, except for the colour scheme of the parts, until it was discontinued in 1992. There is still considerable demand for a Meccano No. 10 set of this red and green period, particularly from older enthusiasts reaching retirement, as the models are a challenge to build and still a joy to behold when well constructed.

In recent years new No. 10 set models have been published by enthusiasts keen to meet the challenge of designing realistic models within the confines of the outfit.

Meccano sales at this time were buoyant and, despite devaluation of the pound in 1948 and the restrictions caused by the Korean War, there was such a high level of demand for Meccano products that the company decided to reduce its expenditure on advertising. This decision may have ultimately contributed to the rapid decline in profits from the high point in 1956 — a decline from which the company never fully recovered.

Opposite, bottom: Meccano outfit No. 0 showing the revised box label.

Below: An accessory set from 1956.

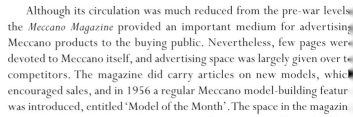

Shop-window
display models
included the
Blackpool Tower
based on the
'Model of the
Month' for
October 1956.

Although its circulation was much reduced from the pre-war levels the *Meccano Magazine* provided an important medium for advertising Meccano products to the buying public. Nevertheless, few pages were devoted to Meccano itself, and advertising space was largely given over to competitors. The magazine did carry articles on new models, which encouraged sales, and in 1956 a regular Meccano model-building feature was introduced, entitled 'Model of the Month'. The space in the magazine was insufficient to allow building instructions, but typed instructions could be obtained free of charge from Binns Road. These models were generally well designed by the Binns Road model room and some were used as shop-window display models for Meccano dealers. These post-war shop display models are very attractive and reminiscent of a bygone age of toy shops laden with Meccano products as seen on the cover of the December 1954 *Meccano Magazine*. Genuine shop display models have also become very desirable as collectors' items.

By the late 1950s a new generation of post-war children was becoming more sophisticated, and the teenage culture revolution had begun. Britain was about to enter the atomic age, and traditional engineering was beginning to lose its attraction as employment opportunities opened in new technologies. Meccano was becoming an old-fashioned toy company to new products such as Lego and plastic construction kits. The company had also lost ground to competitors in other product ranges, particularly its Dinky toys, which now represented almost half of its total sales. Having been the market leader, the company had failed to recognise the need to keep on developing and improving, as it had done successfully before the war.

In order to brighten their image, Meccano sets were repackaged in 19 and new colours were introduced, with most parts finished in lighter shades of red and green. This change of colour scheme was, again, not formally announced and seems to have been introduced gradually from 1958. Not only were the new 1959 boxes brighter, but they featured a model that could actually be built with the outfit. The parts were no longer, irritatingly, especially to impatient youngsters, strung on card but pressed into vacuum-formed plastic trays. However, accessory outfits retained the same cartons as in 1954, with parts still strung onto card.

The two largest sets, Nos. 9 and 10, retained a large element of card-mounted parts. The No. 10 outfit's presentation 'chest' was replaced by a new four-drawer cabinet in lighter oak by 1960, but was available for a short period in either. The No. 9 outfit, previously available in an oak-stained presentation cabinet with one lift-out tray, was now available only in a carton.

A further change in presentation was announced as the 'New' Meccano in early 1962. A few new parts were introduced and the cartons were modified to display the letter 'M' prominently, but the only major change was to the instruction books.

A No. 4 outfit from the 1959–61 range in bright new cartons depicting a model built with the set. Note the manual in bright colour, and the boys without their father and more modern in appearance.

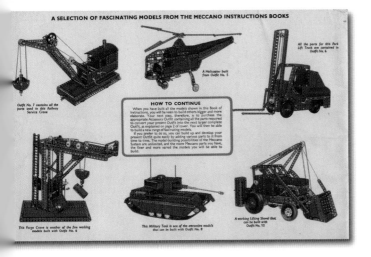

The back cover of 1956–61 Meccano manuals, showing models built with outfits Nos. 5 to 10.

The format of Meccano instruction manuals had hardly changed since the 1930s: models were photographed and described in text that demanded a high level of concentration and reading ability. The new manuals went some way to recognising the change in the boys who were playing with Meccano by showing models in 'exploded' views indicating part numbers but without any written instructions, so making model plans easier to understand for younger boys. The instructions were also easier to modify for foreign editions, and so less costly to produce. Manuals covered set nos 0 to 1, 2 to 3, 4 to 6 and 7 to 8, so all manuals included models for more than one set, and consequently fewer models were provided for each outfit. A new series of ten special model leaflets was introduced for outfit No. 9, but the instruction leaflets for the No. 10 outfit were unchanged.

Supplementary gears outfits, introduced in 1950 as the 'Gears Set A' subsequently modified to 'Gears Set B' in 1956, provided an economic way

Advertisement from the February 1962 *Meccano Magazine* announcing the new Meccano sets and parts.

No. 10 outfit in a new four-drawer cabinet in the new colour scheme, with parts still strung on to card.

o extend the range of models that could be built with main outfit. In 1959 a larger 'Mechanisms' outfit included some standard parts and a very useful manual that contained a good range of mechanisms drawn from the Meccano archives. Many of the mechanisms had previously been featured in the *Meccano Magazine*.

Since the introduction of the No. 10 outfit before the war, Meccano had ignored the potential of electricity; the pre-war electrical outfits and electrical parts, although quite rudimentary, had provided an opportunity to create switches and electro-magnets. In 1963 Meccano introduced its finest ever electrical outfit for use with standard Meccano outfits; the 'Elektrikit', initially designed by Meccano (France) and adapted by Binns Road, included a good range of special electrical parts, including insulating adaptations of standard Meccano parts. A comprehensive manual provided instructions for constructing electrical apparatus including switches, relays and a complete Morse telegraph, although two outfits were needed for this.

Meccano had now re-established its range of standard sets and maintained the quality of its pre-war product. Outfits were well presented, and Meccano still retained its reputation as a quality product that supported the development of engineering skills. However, the world had changed: boys no longer wore short trousers or aspired to be engineers; television and popular culture absorbed the attention of teenagers. Despite some updating of image, Meccano sales did not match up to forecasts, and throughout 1963 Meccano Ltd was getting deeper into financial crisis. By the end of the year Meccano Ltd was facing trading losses of £50,000 and was heavily overdrawn.

The 'Mechanisms' outfit introduced in 1959.

Advertisement from the May 1963 *Meccano Magazine* introducing the Elektrikit, adapted by Meccano's Liverpool factory from a Meccano (France) outfit.

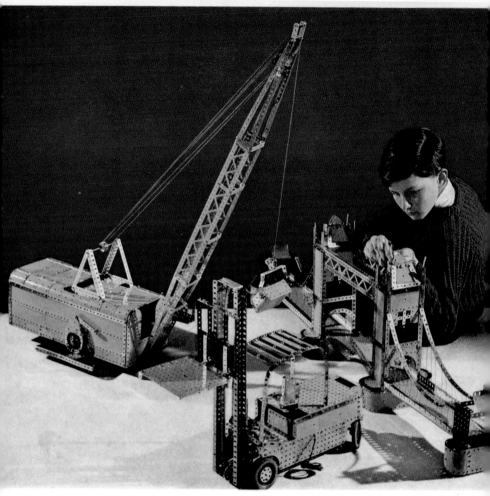

My dad's an engineer - so am I!

You get terrific fun with new-look Meccano—the fun
things that really work! Bridges that cars and soldiers
. . . cranes that *lift* things . . . trucks that *go!*

Every new-look Meccano set contains engineering
giving you details and illustrations of dozens of real-to-
to make. And, of course, you can design and build
yourself.

These are the fabulous sets you can choose from:-
WORK BOX SETS from 14/11 —Playset; Junior Set; Super Junior. And THEN
£1.18.6—No. 3 Highway Vehicles; No. 4 Airport Service; No. 5 Site Engine
Ocean Terminal; No. 7 Mountain Engineer; No. 8 Breakdown Crew; No. 9 Ma

NEW LOO
MECCAN

CCANO LTD. BINNS ROAD. LIVERPOOL.

THE FINAL YEARS: 1964–79

MEETING in February 1964, the Meccano board of directors recommended that shareholders accept an offer from the Lines Group, the owners of Tri-ang Toys, a competitor since the 1920s, to take over Meccano Ltd. Roland Hornby and his sister-in-law, Una (the widow of his brother, Douglas), were removed from the board, and for the first time in over half a century the Hornby family was not in charge of the future of the company. Coincidentally, Walter Lines had once offered to sell his Tri-ang Toys business to Frank Hornby. The Meccano management was replaced by a younger team, which immediately set about restyling the 'famous Meccano model engineering construction system'.

New Meccano sets were announced in August 1964. There was no change contents, but a major change of packaging and colours. The new livery was inspired by the huge construction projects taking place all over Britain the late 1950s and early 1960s, particularly the building of new roads such as the M1 motorway, the first part of which opened in November 1959. The *Meccano Magazine* carried an article explaining the change and the revised colours of silver, yellow and black – 'not only providing a brighter visual appeal but also because these colours are prevalent in the building and engineering world'. Unfortunately the silver paint was poorly applied, often over the previous green, making this the worst and least durable Meccano colour.

Boxes were modified to slip-cases containing a polystyrene tray holding the parts; for outfits Nos. 3 to 8 they carried pictures of models derived from those in the outfit instruction manual. To appeal to younger boys, the Nos. 0, and 2 sets were called respectively the 'Playset', 'Junior' and 'Super Junior' sets and packaged in special carry-case boxes. To appeal to mothers, the parts were held in a 'Meccano-tidy' in 'tool-roll' form, encouraging boys to tidy away their Meccano after dismantling models! The No. 9 set was renamed the Master Engineer's' set, but within the new-style slip-case the set was packaged as the previous red and green sets but with parts in the new colours. The No. 10 set was unchanged apart from the new colour scheme.

Opposite:
Meccano Magazine advertisement for the new Meccano sets, emphasising the realism of models linked with major construction projects under way all over Britain.

Right: The new
names for
Meccano sets
in 1964.

Far right:
Explanation of
the new 1964
colour scheme.

Set No. Meccano sets for 1964

0	Playset
1	Junior set
2	Super Junior set
3	Highway Vehicles set
4	Airport Service set
5	Site Engineering set
6	Ocean Terminal set
7	Mountain Engineer's set
8	Breakdown Crew set
9	Master Engineer's set
10	Oak Cabinet

Old colour: Green / New colour: Silver	3
Old colour: Green / New colour: Silver	9b
Old colour: Red / New colour: Black	52
Old colour: Green / New colour: Silver	55
Old colour: Green / New colour: Nickel	77
Old colour: Green / New colour: Silver	90
Old colour: Green / New colour: Silver	108
Old colour: Red / New colour: Black	109
Old colour: Green / New colour: Silver	160
Old colour: Red / New colour: Black	162
Old colour: Red / New colour: Yellow	198
Old colour: Red / New colour: Yellow	214
Old colour: Red / New colour: Yellow	224

Existing owners of outfits were assured that production of red and green accessory outfits would continue and that spare parts in those colours would also be available 'for some time yet'. In reality Meccano spare parts were now difficult to find in any quantity, especially those exclusive to the No. 10 outfit, and boys who could not afford the very costly No. 9a outfit had little prospect of extending their No. 9 into a 'ten s[...] by weekly purchases from pocket money.

The design of the Meccano electric motors had changed little for alm[...]

The 1964–70
No. 9 set – the old
packaging in a new
slip-case.

orty years. The side-plate motors
eintroduced after the war as the 20-volt
20R, and then the 12–15-volt E15R,
were labour-intensive to produce,
nprofitable, bulky and old-fashioned. In
965 Meccano adopted a West German
motor (the Richard Monoperm), already
esigned for use with Meccano, and added
to the No. 4 outfit to make the Meccano
'ower Drive set.

The Meccano steam engine produced
n 1929 was available for only a few years,
nd no replacement had been possible in
ne post-war years because of the high cost
f production. Mamod (Malins Engineers
f Stafford) produced a range of steam
ngines that were suitable and in 1965
ere persuaded to produce a Meccano
eam engine with reversing gear.

Also in 1965, Meccano Ltd at last
:cognised the need for a Meccano system
iitable for small children and introduced
astic Meccano. Based on the same

The Meccano
Power Drive set
introduced in
August 1965,
in the new-style
packaging.

The 1965 Meccano
steam engine.

This little boy built a smashing 'grab' for fun — with the big, chunky pieces of new Plastic Meccano

Plastic Meccano for younger children came in three sets, A, B and C.

modular principle as metal sets, plastic Meccano had larger nuts and bolts, was easier to manipulate with small hands and consequently proved popular with primary schools. In contrast, Meccano marketing failed to recognise the growing number of adult enthusiasts, despite a large number of entries from adults in Meccano model building competitions, and the constant correspondence from frustrated enthusiasts wanting Meccano spares.

A small group of adult enthusiasts in the Midlands had begun to meet to share experiences of model building in Meccano. Initially called the 'South Midlands Adult Meccano Society', the group expanded and began meeting as the Midlands Meccano Guild in 1967. The Guild was open to all adult Meccano builders, but no upper or lower age limits were fixed, and, in contrast to model engineering societies, it was agreed that

An early meeting in 1965 of what was to become the Midland Meccano Guild. Left to right: Bob Faulkner, Esmond Roden, Jack Partridge, David Goodman, Ernie Chandler, Bert Love and Eric Jenkins.

eneral model building (other than
a Meccano) should be excluded.
argely because of the enthusiasm
f Bert Love, interest in Meccano
lubs was revived, at home and
broad, and as a result many
Meccano societies still thrive today.
he inauguration of the Midlands
Meccano Guild, the first Meccano
lub primarily aimed at adult
membership, was noted in the
elaunched *Meccano Magazine* in
anuary 1968.

The *Meccano Magazine* had
olded in 1967 after fifty-one years
f publication but was relaunched
nder new ownership. In a
eparture from previous practice,
ticles were invited from Meccano
nthusiasts. However, the
rculation did not achieve
fficiently high levels to ensure its
ong-term viability and the
agazine closed down again in

Cover of the
revived *Meccano
Magazine* showing
a boy working on
what was a
popular dealer
display model,
the No. 10 set
showman's
traction engine.

72, to be resurrected as a quarterly, again published by Meccano Ltd. It
ntinued in publication until 1981.

With the 'new look' Meccano, 'accessory sets' were more accurately
named 'conversion sets', repacked in smaller boxes with parts no longer
ntained in plastic trays. By the 1966–7 season the aluminium paint was
placed by zinc plating of strips and girders, and the larger conversion sets,
and 9a, were no longer included in price lists.

A promotional booklet, *Meccano and the Story of Toys*, published in 1968,
phasised the worldwide interest in Meccano, commenting on models sent
the Liverpool factory

> … from inventors all over the world, including some very cleverly designed
> [models], like the ingenious walking horse and chariot from Hungary, an
> automatic clock that accurately registers hours, minutes and seconds from
> a builder in Italy, a working Shay steam locomotive from Germany…

any of these were entries in model-building competitions. The booklet also
nt on:

MECCANO

AND
THE STORY OF
TOYS

Meccano promotional booklet from 1968 – a contrast to the high-quality colour booklets of the pre-war era.

Sir Alec Issigonis depicted in a Meccano promotional leaflet in 1971, and the No. 10 Meccano set such as he received as a retirement gift.

Sir Alec Issigonis

designer of the British Leyland Mini and Morris Minor, has been a Meccano fan for most of his life. So much of a fan, in fact, that as a retirement present British Leyland gave him what is every boy's dream— a Meccano No. 10 Set.

Although Meccano makes an ideal toy, it has more serious uses. Among the companies that use Meccano to aid them in research and development projects are the United Kingdom Atomic Energy Authority, the British Aircraft Corporation and the Atomic Weapons Research Establishment at Aldermaston.

The standard and quality of Meccano modelling was as high as ever. However, its versatility as both an instructional toy and an engineering design tool, used, for example, in the design of the Mini by Sir Alec Issigonis, would soon be superseded by the advent of computer-aided design systems.

9 and 10—the big sets—for the boy who has everything!

The sets every boy dreams of owning! The De Luxe No. 9 set has*1,220 parts, the Grand De Luxe No. 10 set nearly*3,000! Both come in handsome oak finished cabinets, and provide tremendous scope for inventive minds. Literally hundreds and hundreds of terrific working models can be built. *Including nuts and bolts.

Since the end of the Second World War Meccano production in Paris had continued using the pre-war livery of blue and gold, although not in exactly the same shades as from Meccano, Liverpool. In 1970 an agreement was reached to harmonise the colour schemes produced by Liverpool and Paris with the introduction of a completely new range of Meccano sets. The range of sets was reduced by dropping the existing Master Engineer's (No. 9) set and renumbering sets from 1 to 9, instead of 0 to 9, so that the old set 0 became the new No. 1 set, and so on. This meant reduced prices for Meccano sets but an even bigger jump to the No. 10 set. Nevertheless, despite a low volume of sales, the No. 10 set continued in production. The new colour scheme continued the zinc plating of strips and girders but introduced a new, brighter yellow for plates; the black

The range of sets produced from 1970 to 1977, from a 1975 publicity leaflet.

Space-age brochure promoting the new Meccano range for 1970, though no space-themed sets would be produced for nearly ten years.

parts were recoloured in bright blue – these colours turned out to be not quite the same as the new French yellow and blue.

New manuals were produced for sets Nos. 2 to 7, and a new leaflet for set 1. A few additional parts were also added to the sets. The new manuals provided a range of new models, shown in colour for the first time, and those covering sets Nos. 2 to 4 and 5 to 7 included models making use of a new range of electronic parts. The manuals for the new Nos. 8 and 9 sets (old Nos. 7 and 8) were reprints of the former 7 and 8 manuals and, as with all the new manuals, the covers were plain, with no pictures.

In July 1969 man had made his first landing on the moon, but it would take Meccano ten years to catch up with the space age. A 1970 brochure promoting the new range proclaimed that Meccano had entered the space age, but announced merely the introduction of the electronic control set. This included a new photo-electric cell and a useful 12-volt DC relay enabling automatic control of electric motors. A range of new special sets was also advertised, the most interesting being the 4E, combining set No. 4 with the Elektrikit, and the 5ME, combining set No. 5 with the electronic control set and including the 6–12-volt power-drive motor. Although reasonably priced at £8.95 and £11.95, these sets were not popular; the 5ME set was £2.00 more expensive than the No. 8 set.

The close association of Bert Love with the editorial team of the *Meccano Magazine*, and his regular contribution of articles on modelling and the history of Meccano, brought an increased awareness of the strength of adult enthusiasm for Meccano. In 1970 Meccano models built by Bob Moy, in charge of building display models at Binns Road, and Meccano enthusiasts were displayed at the Model Engineering Exhibition in London and attracted much interest from exhibitors and the public. Bert Love reported in the *Meccano Magazine* the public reaction to his giant block-setting crane:

> Fathers and grandfathers lingered to reminisce over their ambitions to build a similar model in their youth and many were encouraged to look out their old stocks of Meccano with a view to returning to this wonderful hobby.

Meccano models are today a regular feature of model engineering exhibitions.

In 1971 Meccano Ltd survived the liquidation of its parent company, Lines Brothers Group, largely through the timely action of its managing director, Joe Fallman, and re-emerged as Meccano (1971), acquired by Airfix Industries, while General Mills Corporation of the United States acquired Meccano's French operation.

In the following six six years, to 1977, a wealth of new and generally successful Meccano construction sets was developed, beginning with two novel weight-driven clocks in 1972. Meccano clocks had frequently been prizewinners in competitions, including in 1915, despite the lack of suitable gears to provide any degree of accuracy. The No. 1 clock kit advertised in May 1972 was a simple weight-driven clock similar in design to a model featured in an earlier *Meccano Magazine*. Although inexpensive at £4.00, it was a crude design that did not work well. The No. 2 clock kit was more sophisticated and included a complex chiming device for striking the hours, but it was difficult to build and did not achieve the hoped-for volume of sales. However, at just over £8.00 it was a bargain for Meccano enthusiasts, including a wealth of expensive gears and parts, all of which were extremely difficult to find as spare parts. Producing these single-model Meccano sets requiring specialised parts marked a change from the philosophy of providing only general-purpose sets with standard parts.

Much more successful was the range of Multi kits – particularly the Army Multi kit and the smaller Army Combat kit, which was voted by the trade as runner-up to the 'Best Boy's Toy of the Year'. The Army and Highway Multi kits, introduced in 1973, were given excellent new manuals

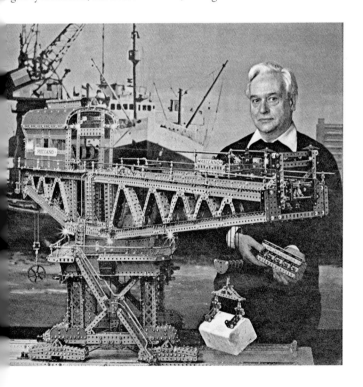

Bert Love and a much-mproved version of the giant block-setting crane, from an article in the *Observer* colour supplement in 1969.

Multi kits first
introduced in 1973
and shown here
from a 1975
advertisement.

which did away with the difficult-to-follow exploded views and instead
provided step-by-step colour photographs of how the models are
constructed. These manuals are among the best ever produced, including
realistic and attractive new models. The Army Multi kit also exploited the
potential play value of models such as the missile launcher, which would
actually fire a missile, and the shell-firing light tank. In 1975 the range was
extended to include the Super-Highway and the smaller Combat Multi
kit. A new small DC electric motor, based on an imported Mabuchi
4.5-volt unit, was introduced in 1976 and included in a 'Crane-Building
Set' Multi kit. The new Multi kits proved so successful that the factory at
Binns Road could not cope with the demand for the range of new outfits
as well as supplying spare parts to its dealers.

Meccano nuts had remained unchanged since Frank Hornby invented
Mechanics Made Easy some seventy years earlier. In 1973 the square
$^5/_{32}$-inch BSW thread nut was replaced by a hexagonal nut still of the same
thread, and these nuts were gradually introduced across the range of sets
starting with the new Multi kits. Zinc coating, rather than brass, had been
used for nuts and bolts since 1964.

In 1977 a superficial change was made to the presentation of sets, with
new carton lids depicting both boys and girls building Meccano models.
'unisex' presentation had been quickly abandoned by Frank Hornby in 1926
and this latest attempt proved to be equally short-lived because of a total
reorganisation of the Meccano range for 1978.

The company was now entering the final years of production at Binns Road. The ravages of inflation brought about by massive price increases in raw materials and decimalisation, unreasonable wage demands and persistent labour relations problems all contributed to the company's ultimate failure. Most of the equipment was by now antiquated, resulting in high volumes of waste material, and what changes were made in the production equipment could not achieve the increased efficiency now needed. There were also significant changes in the management; perhaps the most successful post-war managing director, Joe Fallman, had resigned in 1975, and by 1977 the marketing director, Doug McHard, had also moved on.

A set 4M from the short-run standard range of Meccano sets for 1977.

Sets from the range introduced in 1978 in the new colours of dark blue and mustard yellow.

The new company management came to the conclusion that a radical new approach was needed to reduce production costs and bring Meccano up to date. For 1978 zinc plating was abandoned and replaced by a dark blue enamel sets ceased to be progressive, and the range was drastically cut. The content of sets Nos. 1 to 5 were completely revised and linked by only two 'extension sets: an 'S' (small) pack extending set No. 1 or 2 into set No. 3, and an 'L (large) pack to extend a No. 3 or 4 set into a No. 5 set. Each of the new set from No. 2 to No. 5 was motorised by the 4½-volt motor, with parts held in a somewhat larger than necessary polystyrene tray. The No. 2 clock kit and the Super-Highway sets were discontinued. Sets Nos. 9 and 10 were retained but with significant price increases: in 1975 the No. 10 Meccano set had increased in price to £192, and by 1978 it cost an eye-watering £300. Although no changes were made to the contents of the No. 10 set, some economies were made by no longer sewing the parts onto card and using a cheaper, three drawer cabinet. As a result, most parts were loosely contained in moulded plastic trays.

An example of a late No. 10 set produced in 1978–9 in a three-drawer cabinet with plastic trays in which parts were loosely contained.

There were no changes to the model instructions for sets Nos. 9 and 10 but each of the new sets Nos. 1 to 5 was accompanied by a new book of models.

The last No. 10 sets produced by the Binns Road factory in 1979 had many anomalies resulting from inclusion of the previous instruction leaflets and old manuals as well as the new books of models for Nos. 1 to 5. Parts required for some models were no longer included, and the E15R motor was no longer available. At the cost of £350, the No. 10 set was out of reach to all but the

The last Meccano products developed at Binns Road before closure in 1980 – single-model 'pocket-money' Action Packs.

most affluent, and consequently achieved a very low volume of sales and was completely uneconomic to produce.

In an attempt to establish a modern image for Meccano, a range of 'space' sets was introduced in 1979, ten years after the first manned moon landing in July 1969. Meccano had used the term 'space age' since 1970 but had produced no specific space-related Meccano sets. In a move to keep costs low, the new sets contained a larger proportion of plastic parts. Added realism was achieved by special parts for the nose cone and cockpit canopy, and the inclusion of a diecast missile launcher provided extra play value. The Meccanoids set (Meccano In Deepest Space) was a fantasy set for building space monsters. Unfortunately several errors were made in the design of the models so that, when built to the instructions, they were both unstable and underpowered and did not work properly.

The last product to be developed by Meccano Ltd at Liverpool was a range of 'pocket-money' sets aimed at impulse sales in supermarkets. 'Action Packs' featured an easy-to-build topical 'mini' model with an action feature such as firing a missile. Three series were available, with larger models making up series 2 and 3 and including a novel clockwork motor. These sets also made extensive use of plastic.

On Friday 30 November 1979 Meccano Ltd announced the closure of the Binns Road factory in Liverpool. Attempts by the workforce to prevent permanent closure resulted only in a period of delay to the inevitable winding up of Meccano Ltd. The company had run out of cash to pay its bills, had an overdraft of several million pounds, and had no prospect of resurrecting the successes of the past in a changed market and a society looking to new technologies for its playthings. Despite this ultimate failure of the company, the production of Meccano, which began in 1908, had lasted over seventy years, gave rise to numerous imitations worldwide, and remains part of the heritage of the nation as the 'toy that made engineering famous'.

Meccano 'Space' sets, developed at Binns Road in 1979.

SPACE 2501 AND MECCANOIDS

POSTSCRIPT: AFTER 1980

MECCANO is an enduring product and, despite the failure of Meccano Ltd in 1979, production of Meccano has continued since then under various ownerships. Following the closure of the Binns Road factory, production was continued by the new American owners, General Mills, at the Meccano (France) factory in Calais. The existing product range was scrapped and a much reduced range of Meccano sets 1000, 2000 and 3000 was introduced. After General Mills sold its toy interests, and following a year-long closure of the Meccano factory at Calais, there was a further change of ownership in 1985 to Marc Rebibo, resulting in a relaunch of a more traditional range of Meccano, sets Nos. 1 to 6. In 1989 Meccano France became an independent company and bought the rights to the Erector trademark in the United States. In 2000 Meccano France was sold to the Japanese company Nikko, and and since 2007 is mainly been owned by Alain Ingberg. Although still produced in Calais, these changes in ownership have led to radically different products and marketing. Meccano outfits are now designed around the construction of a single model and have ceased to be general-purpose outfits. With this change, the concept of a range of standard parts has largely been abandoned and new special-purpose parts are designed specifically for each new outfit. Most of the parts exclusive to the No. 10 set, eagerly desired by boys in the 1950s, are no longer produced. However, the Meccano standard spacing of half inch and the use of $^5/_{32}$-inch Whitworth bolts continues despite their obsolescence in the real world of engineering.

Meccano is today a hobby pursued mostly by adults, some of whom are former 'Meccano boys' who, on reaching retirement, have time to devote to a pastime they enjoyed as children.

Meccano was exported around the world, gave rise to many similar construction toys, and still has a worldwide following. Replica parts are manufactured

Meccano in 1994 was still a starting point for a career in engineering.

to replace those once available in the traditional No. 10 set. However, more than seventy years of production have provided a wealth of Meccano parts that can be found at every car boot sale and on internet auction sites. The consistent use of the standard half-inch spacing enables those parts, no matter how old, to be still of use even today.

The official Meccano Guild no longer exists, having largely disappeared by 1965, but there is still a healthy membership of Meccano clubs around the world, and an International Society of Meccanomen, which promotes dialogue between national clubs and provides a rich source of new model and literature. Most clubs produce a club magazine, and some of these magazines have developed into commercially viable publications such as

Constructor Quarterly. Enthusiasts have further developed the range of model plans based on the traditional No. 10 set, and new plans are published constantly.

Meccano, the toy that created a business empire and made Frank Hornby's Liverpool company the most successful British toy manufacturer of the twentieth century, is today still used for the purpose that its originator intended – to help young and old develop and understand the principles of engineering and build things that really work. For the thousands of adult 'Meccanomen' who still use Meccano it has been a lifelong enthusiasm. Meccano was 'the toy that grows with the boy', and for many it was the toy that developed the skills that gave them successful careers as engineers.

An impressive Meccano model by John Thorpe which won first prize and the Issigonis Shield at the international Meccano exhibition in Skegness in 2006.

CHRONOLOGY OF MECCANO

1863 Frank Hornby born (15 May).

1901 Hornby produces and patents 'Mechanics Made Easy'; sets A and B produced with tin-plated parts.

1907 'Meccano' name registered (14 September).

1908 First 'Meccano' sets produced, sets 1–6 in nickel-plate.

1912 Meccano (France) founded.

1914 Binns Road factory, Liverpool, opened.

1916 *Meccano Magazine* first issued.

1919 Meccano Guild established (with Frank Hornby as President).

1922 No. 7 set introduced. Meccano factory opens in New Jersey, USA.

1926 'New Meccano' introduced, some parts painted light red and green.

1927 Colour scheme revised, most parts painted darker red and green.

1931 Aeroplane Constructor sets introduced.

1932 Motor Car Constructor sets introduced.

1934 Meccano range revised (sets A–L). Blue and gold colour scheme.

1936 Frank Hornby dies aged seventy-three (21 September).

1937 Meccano range revised: sets 0–10. Blue and gold colour scheme retained.

1941 Meccano production ceased during Second World War.

1945 First post-war sets produced in medium red and green painted finish.

1958 Lighter shades of red and green gradually replaced the previous medium shades.

1964 Meccano Ltd taken over by Lines Brothers (Tri-ang). Colour scheme changed to black, yellow and silver.

1967 Colour scheme revised to yellow, blue and zinc plate

1970 Change in colour shades to conform with Meccano (France) blue, yellow and zinc plate.

1971 Lines Brothers in liquidation. Meccano Ltd bought by Airfix.

1973 Multi kits introduced.

1978 Range of standard sets reduced to Nos. 1–5, No. 9 and No. 10, in dark blue and mustard yellow colours.

1979 Binns Road factory closes (30 November). Production of Meccano continued in France.

1980 French production continues in 1970s, colour scheme blue, yellow and zinc plate.

1981 *Meccano Magazine* ceases publication.

FURTHER
INFORMATION

MECCANO CLUBS AND SOCIETIES

Although the Meccano Guild no longer exists formally, there are still many Meccano clubs and societies that still use this title. Some have a long history that connects them with the Meccano Guild administered by Meccano Ltd. Meccano societies may be found throughout the world and many can be located from the Meccanowebring on the internet at www.meccanonut.com/meccring.

Societies referred to in this publication are:
International Society of Meccanomen:
   www.internationalmeccanomen.org.uk
Midlands Meccano Guild (MMG): www.midlandsmeccanoguild.com

FURTHER READING

Beardsley, R. *The Hornby Companion*. New Cavendish Books, 1992.
Brown, Kenneth D. *Factory of Dreams. A History of Meccano Ltd*. Carnegie Press, 2008.
Constructor Quarterly. Published by Robin Johnson, 17 Ryegate Road, Crosspool, Sheffield S10 5FA. www.constructorquarterly.com
Gamble, Jim. *Frank Hornby Notes and Pictures*. James G. Gamble, Nottingham, 2001.
Gould, M. P. *Frank Hornby – The Boy Who Made $1,000,000 with a Toy*. New York, 1915.
Ensley, Hubert. *My Meccano Days*. Constructor Quarterly, 1994.
Love, B., and Gamble, J. *The Meccano System and Special Purpose Meccano Sets*. New Cavendish Books, 1986.
Randall, P. *The Products of Binns Road: A General Survey*. New Cavendish Books, 1977.
Wright, G. *The Meccano Super Models*. New Cavendish Books, 1978.

INDEX

Page numbers in italics refer to illustrations